W9-BUE-857

the BEST LITTLE BOOK of One Liners

Compiled by Henny Youngman

RUNNING PRESS   Philadelphia • London

A Running Press Miniature Edition™

Copyright © 1992 by Henny Youngman.
Printed in China.
All rights reserved under the Pan-American and International
Copyright Conventions.

Library of Congress Cataloging-in-Publication Number
92–53813
ISBN 1–56138–180–2

This book may be ordered by mail from the publisher. Please include
$1.00 for postage and handling. But try your bookstore first!
Running Press Book Publishers
125 South Twenty-second Street
Philadelphia, Pennsylvania 19103

a guy came up to me and said he'd bet me fifty dollars that I was dead. I was afraid to take the bet."

The "I" in that joke ain't me— he's an *alter kocker*.

Alter kocker is an important phrase for everyone over forty to know, no matter what business you're in. Literally, it's Yiddish for old shi...oh, never mind what it literally means. I've always worked a clean act.

In show business, an *alter kocker* is an old guy who was once a player in the industry, but who now sits around telling the same goddam story to whoever will listen about the time he played polo with Sam Goldwyn, Clark Gable, and Gummo Marx. In life, being an *alter kocker* means that you've closed up shop, put your brain in the closet, decided that you're happier thinking about what happened yesterday than figuring out what's going to happen tomorrow.

I'm no *alter kocker*. That's why when the kid comics come up to my Friars Club table and say, "Mr. Youngman, how old *are* you?" I don't tell them I'm eighty-six. That's just a number, it doesn't mean anything. Instead, I tell them a joke.

"I'm so old," I say, "that when I order a three-minute egg here, they make me pay up front."

They usually laugh, and to me, that means everything. I tried smart comedy once, but people wouldn't believe it from a guy like me. I play for the masses. My jokes happen to everybody.

Some people get embarrassed because my jokes are corn. They're plain, but for over sixty years they've made people laugh. And if I can still make someone laugh, then I still must be alive.

Henny

I take my wife everywhere, but she always finds her way home.

I haven't talked to my wife in three weeks. I didn't want to interrupt her.

You meet the craziest people on the subway. One guy sitting next to me kept saying, "Call me a doctor—call me a doctor!"

I asked, "What's the matter, are you sick?"

He said, "No, I just graduated from medical school."

Be careful when you're speaking about him—you're speaking of the man he loves.

A fellow goes to a psychiatrist. The psychiatrist says, "You're crazy."

The guy says, "I want a second opinion."

The psychiatrist answers, "You're ugly too!"

*Y*ou should have been born in the Dark Ages—you sure look awful in the light.

*S*he got her good looks from her father. He's a plastic surgeon.

I like you—I have no taste, but I like you.

a doctor said to a little old man, "You're going to live until you're sixty."

He said, "I am sixty."

The doctor said, "What did I tell you?"

a nurse says to a doctor, "The man you just gave a clean bill of health dropped dead outside your office door."

The doctor says, "Turn him around—make believe he's coming in."

♪'ve got a great doctor. He gave a guy six months to live. The guy couldn't pay his bill so my doctor gave him another six months.

♪ went up to visit my doctor with a sore foot. He said, "I'll have you walking in an hour."

He did. He stole my car.

I solved the parking problem—I bought a parked car.

*N*eurotic: A person who worries about things that didn't happen in the past, instead of worrying about something that won't happen in the future—like normal people.

I call my lawyer and say, "Can I ask you two questions?"

My lawyer says, "What's the second question?"

The other day a policeman stopped me going the wrong way on a one-way street. He said, "Didn't you see the arrow?"

I said, "Arrow? Honestly, Officer, I didn't even see the Indians."

Wild flowers fade fast, but blooming idiots last forever.

Camp Hiawatha, Camp Seneca—that's where the Jewish kids go for the summer.

Who goes to Camp Ginsburg?

What do you call a Jewish baby who isn't circumcised? A girl!

Show me a Jewish boy who doesn't go to medical school and I'll show you a lawyer.

A fellow asks, "Can I park here?"

The cop tells him no, and the fellow says, "What about the other cars?"

The cop answers, "They didn't ask!"

After the show could I drop you off somewhere? Say—the roof?

Your Early American features fascinate me—you look like a buffalo.

Tell me, is that your lower lip, or are you wearing a turtleneck?

Two guys are in a gym and one puts on a girdle.

"Since when have you been wearing a girdle?" says one guy.

"Since my wife found it in the glove compartment," says the other.

He's frank and earnest with women. In Chicago he's Frank and in New York he's Ernest.

A fellow walks into a bank and says, "Give me all your money!"

The manager says, "Take the books too, I'm $10,000 short!"

A guy dies and leaves the shortest will ever. It says, "Being of sound mind, I spent my money!"

*N*ow that I've learned to make the most of life, most of it is gone.

*N*ow that he's made his mark in the world, he wants to learn to write his full name.

*W*hy don't you become a dart-licker for the headhunters?

*Y*ou're going over like a pregnant woman doing a pole-vault.

A panhandler said to me, "Mister, I haven't tasted food for a week."
I said, "Don't worry, it still tastes the same."

A panhandler walked up to me and said, "I haven't had a bite all day."

So I bit him.

I'm a light eater.

As soon as it gets light, I start eating.

a guy says to me, "Do you know where Central Park is?"

I said, "No."

He says, "O.K., I'll mug you here."

I once thought of becoming an atheist, but I changed my mind; no paid holidays.

*W*hen Moses sat on top of Mt. Sinai, you know what he really said?

"This would be a good place for a hospital."

It will be tough getting along without you, but let me try.

Next time you pass my house, I'd appreciate it.

It's getting to the point where you need more brains to make out the income tax forms than to make the income.

I just finished filling out my income tax form. Who said you can't get wounded by a blank?

*L*et's play house. You be the door and I'll slam you.

*Y*ou must come out to my swimming pool so I can give you drowning lessons.

*Y*ou may have been born with a silver spoon in your mouth—but I bet it had someone else's initials on it.

*W*hen a guy says he's fixed for life, you don't know whether he's talking about a pension or a vasectomy.

Remember when "Charge!" meant the Light Brigade instead of Diner's Club?

He's the kind of guy who would ask for separate checks at the Last Supper.

My wife just had plastic surgery. I cut up her credit cards.

My wife will buy anything marked down.

She just bought two dresses and an escalator.

She's very partial to that dress. She wears it when she wants to look halfway decent—but not completely.

You make that dress look ten years younger.

This woman dresses to kill. I understand she cooks the same way.

Payday at my house is like the Academy Awards. My wife says, "May I have the envelope, please?"

I've been married for fifty years and I'm still in love with the same woman. If my wife ever finds out she'll kill me.

If your wife doesn't treat you right, stay with her anyway. There's no better way of punishing her.

There's only one thing that keeps her from being a happily married woman—him.

My wife and I were considering a divorce, but after pricing lawyers we decided to buy a new car instead.

Want to have some fun? Walk into an antique shop and say, "What's new?"

There's a bus leaving in five minutes—get under it.

If you had known yesterday what you know now, you would have been an idiot then, too.

Scientifically, it would be wrong to call him an idiot. He can clothe himself and perform simple tasks—so he's a moron.

Some people stay longer when they're leaving than others do when they're staying.

Neiman Marcus is very good to their customers. A woman broke her leg, and they had it gift wrapped.

When a little girl says, "I'm a girl and you're a boy," and the boy says, "I'll go ask my mother," that's research. When he says, "Let's see," that's sex.

I still love the oldie about the convict who was going to die in the electric chair and called his lawyer for some advice.

The barrister replied, "Don't sit down!"

A lawyer is swimming in the water. A shark comes toward him and veers away—professional courtesy.

He's nobody's fool—he's a free-lancer.

I always like to think the best of people. That's why I consider you an idiot.

*J*ury: A group of twelve people selected to decide who has a better lawyer.

*P*sychiatrist: A doctor who can't stand the sight of blood.

*F*aculty: The people who get what's left after the football coach receives his salary.

I have a very fine doctor. If you can't afford the operation, he touches up the X rays.

My arm started to hurt me. I said, "Doctor, examine my arm."

He looked at my arm, brought out a medical book, and studied it for fifteen minutes.

Then he said to me, "Have you ever had that pain before?"

I said, "Yes."

"Well," he replied, "You've got it again."

My doctor examined this little old lady and told her, "Madam, that is the ugliest body I have ever seen."

She said, "Frankly, that's what my regular doctor told me."

He said, "Why did you come to me?"

"I wanted another opinion," she replied.

I went to my doctor last week and he told me to take a hot bath before retiring. But that's ridiculous. It'll be years before I retire.

Even when my mother was 88 years old she never used glasses— drank right out of the bottle.

My father was never home; he was always drinking booze. He saw a sign saying, "Drink Canada Dry!" So he went up there to do it.

One year, my brother went into the breeding business. He tried to cross a rooster with a rooster.

You know what he got? A very cross rooster.

He's such a phony that he gets cavities in his false teeth.

He has so little personality—he worked on a color television show and came out in black and white.

$\mathcal{L}$et's play Building and Loan. Just get out of the building and leave me alone.

$\mathcal{A}$ furrier crossed a mink and a gorilla. Beautiful fur coat, but the sleeves are too long.

$\mathscr{I}$f they can make penicillin out of moldy bread, surely they can make something out of you.

$\mathscr{I}$ can read you like a book, but it's unfortunate that I can't shut you up like one.

$\mathscr{Y}$ou could be worse. You could be twins.

I know you can't be two-faced or you wouldn't be wearing that one.

A terrorist sent a guy to blow up a car. He burnt his lips on the exhaust pipe.

My grandson, 22 years old, keeps complaining about headaches.

I've told him 1,000 times, "Larry, when you get out of bed, it's feet first."

I asked my grandson, "What are you doing for a living now?"

He said, "I'm a Momback."

I asked, "What's a Momback?"

He said, "I stand behind a truck and holler, 'Momback!'"

Now my grandson's got a new job. He's a lifeguard in a car wash.

Mixed emotions: What you have when your kids borrow ten dollars from you to buy Father's Day presents.

$\mathcal{M}$y brother-in-law is an idiot. During a blackout in New York, he was stuck on an escalator for four hours.

I asked him, "Why didn't you walk down?"

He said, "I was on my way up."

I asked my brother-in-law why he was wearing my raincoat. He answered, "You wouldn't want me to get your suit wet, would you?"

*T*wo dumb guys go bear hunting. They see a sign saying, "Bear left," so they go home.

*H*aving a hole in the head doesn't always indicate an open mind.

Once, a mugger put a gun in my back. He said, "Stick 'em up."

I said, "Stick what up?"

He said, "Don't confuse me. This is my first job."

A lot of people are desperate today. A fellow walked up to me and said, "You see a cop around here?"

I said, "No."

He said, "Stick 'em up!"

I said, "Doc, my foot hurts—what'll I do?"

He said, "Limp."

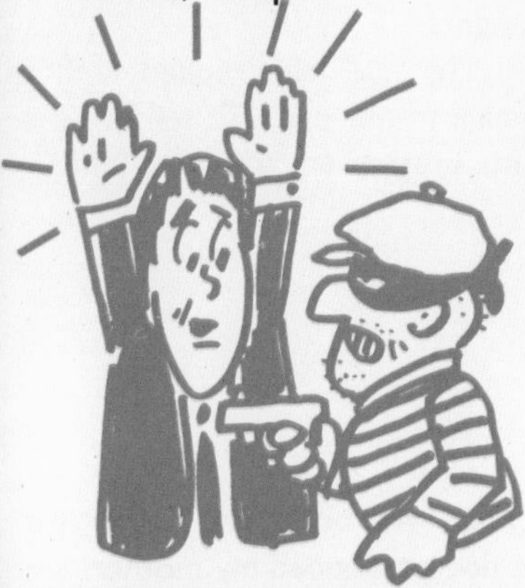

$\mathcal{A}$ cute young woman was consulting a psychiatrist. The doctor asked, "Are you troubled at all by indecent thoughts?"

"Why no," she replied with a twinkle in her eye. "To tell you the truth, I rather enjoy them."

$\mathcal{W}$hen I was born, I was so ugly that the doctor slapped my mother.

Two little boys in Hollywood were exchanging taunts.

"My father can beat your father."

"Oh, yeah? My father *is* your father."

The unabashed dictionary defines adolescence as the age between puberty and adultery.

Things were rough when I was a baby—no talcum powder.

Have you noticed how many more twins are being born these days?

I think that kids are getting afraid to come into this world alone.

A brother-in-law of mine had nine children, so he decided to have a vasectomy. He had it done at Sears. Now, every time he makes love, the garage door opens.

*V*asectomy means never having to say you're sorry.

*M*y wife and I have been married for fifty years. We went back to the same hotel where we got married and had the same suite of rooms—only this time, *I* went into the bathroom and cried.

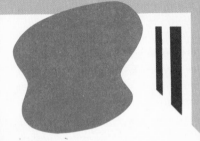

Some people ask the secret of our long marriage. We take time to go to a restaurant twice a week—a little candlelight, dinner, soft music, and dancing.

She goes Tuesdays; I go Fridays.

Do you know what it means to come home at night to a woman who'll give you a little love, a little affection, and a little tenderness?

It means you're in the wrong house.

A woman who never gets taken anywhere by her husband says, "What would it take for you to go on a second honeymoon?"

He says, "A second wife!"

She spends her winters in Florida, springs in California—and falls everywhere.

Somebody asked me, "Henny, do you like bathing beauties?"

I said, "I don't know. I've never bathed one."

You look outstanding; like you've been out standing under a drain pipe.

I don't recall your face—but your breath is familiar.

Strip poker is the only game in which the more you lose, the more you have to show for it.

In Las Vegas, a man said to his wife, "Give me the money I told you not to give me."

He has more talent in his little finger—than he has in his big finger.

He has a sympathetic face; it has everyone's sympathy.

One word you never hear in my house is divorce. Murder, yes, but divorce, no.

Take it like a man—blame it on your wife.

Jaws reminds me of my wife. Once, she avoided being bitten by a shark—she opened her mouth first.

*W*hy do divorces cost so much? They're worth it!

*I*t's a mighty good thing for your wife that you're not married.

A Hollywood couple got divorced, and then remarried—the divorce didn't work out.

$\mathcal{A}$ wife told her husband that the doctor said she wasn't well and needed the ocean breezes. So he fanned her with a herring.

$\mathcal{I}$ have property in Las Vegas. Caesar's Palace has my luggage.

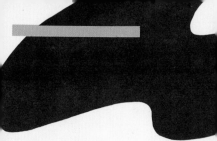

$\mathcal{S}$ome people play a horse to win, some to place. I should have bet this horse to live.

$\mathcal{I}$ made a killing in the market. I shot my broker!

Personally, I detest gambling. I'm so dead set against gambling, I'll bet you 2 to 1 they'll never legalize it!

Anything goes tonight and you may be the first.

There's only one thing wrong with you. You're visible.

I think the world of you—and you know what I think of the world.

*I*n New York's Garment District, a little old man was hit by a car. While waiting for an ambulance, the policeman tucked a blanket under the guy's chin and asked, "Are you comfortable?"

The man said, "I make a nice living."

*S*omeday you'll go too far—and I hope you stay there.

*Y*ou'd make a perfect stranger.

*Y*ou do have one redeeming feature—mortality.

A man brags about his new hearing aid.

"It's the most expensive one I've ever had; it cost $2,500."

His friend asks, "What kind is it?"

He says, "Half-past four!"

New York is so crowded, to get over on the other side of the street, you have to be born there.

The only way you would ever be worth anything is if people were sold by the pound.

The traffic situation in New York is just impossible. I was telling one cop this morning, "You're giving me a ticket for parking? You should give me a medal!"

I checked into my San Francisco hotel room, opened the drawer, and there it was; Tony Bennett's heart.

I guess he left it there.

C ould you believe I used to play at Carnegie Hall—till the cops chased me away.

$\mathcal{W}$ant to get a guy crazy? Send him a telegram saying, "Ignore first wire."

$\mathcal{D}$on't these grand **sunny** summer days make you wish you were alive?

I'd go to the end of the earth for you—if you were at the other end.

One of the members dropped dead at our country club. Nobody wanted to tell his wife, so the doctor said he'd do it.

He called and said, "Mrs. Cohen, your husband Sam lost $500 playing cards at the club."

The wife yelled, "He should drop dead."

The doctor said, "He did."

$\mathcal{W}$hy do guys die before their wives? They want to!

$\mathcal{S}$he has the knack of making strangers immediately.

$\mathcal{S}$he has long flowing blond hair—from each nostril.

She's had her face lifted so many times that she has to walk on tiptoes.

When you go into a restaurant, always ask for a table near a waiter.

The towels in that ritzy hotel were so big and fluffy you could hardly close your suitcase.

Business was so bad the other night that the orchestra was playing "Tea for One."

The other day I found a man's hand in my pocket. I said, "What do you want?"

He said, "I want a match."

I said, "Why didn't you ask for it?"

He said, "I don't talk to strangers."

I told my mother-in-law to take a trip to the Thousand Islands. I told her, "Spend a week in each island!"

I bought my mother-in-law a chair, but they won't let me plug it in.

*K*now what I got for **Father's** Day? The bills from Mother's **Day**.

*W*hen you become a **mother** will you let me adopt one **of the** kittens?

I bought my wife a **car**. Three weeks ago she learned **how** to drive it. Last week, she **learned** how to aim it.

My wife wanted a foreign convertible. I bought her a rickshaw.

Do you know what mixed emotions are? When you see your mother-in-law go over a cliff in your new Cadillac!

I'm just back from a pleasure trip. I took my mother-in-law to the airport.

Have you noticed that most people who give up smoking substitute something for it? Irritability!

He's had his nose broken in two places.

He ought to stay out of those places.

My doctor says I must give up those little intimate dinners for two—unless I have someone eating with me.

I miss my wife's cooking—as often as I can.

I don't mind my wife giving me all those TV dinners, but when she starts heating up the leftovers and calling them re-runs . . .

I'd like to see you starring in a funeral plot.

Don't try and judge her by her clothes—there isn't enough evidence.

That's a very cute dress she almost has on.

*y*our dress is too short. It only extends up to your neck.

*M*y wife called me. She said, "There's water in the carburetor.

I said, "Where's the car?"

She said, "In the lake."

*M*y wife and I had an argument. She wanted to buy a fur coat. I wanted to buy a car. We compromised; we bought a fur coat and keep it in the garage.

*S*he had a coming-out party—but they made her go back in again.

A woman shot her husband with a bow and arrow. She didn't want to wake up the kids.

𝒶 woman wrapped herself in Saran Wrap to take weight off. Her husband came home, saw her, and said, "Left-overs again!"

𝔞 came home last night and found a car in the dining room.

I said to my wife, "How did you get the car in the dining room?"

She said, "It was easy. I made a left turn when I came out of the kitchen."

$\mathcal{W}$e were married for better or worse. I couldn't have done better and she couldn't have done worse.

$\mathcal{M}$y wife saw the garbagemen leaving our house. She shouted, "Am I too late for the garbage?"

They answered, "No, jump in!"

We went for a ride and my wife went through a red light. I said, "Didn't you see that red light?"

She said, "You see one red light, you've seen them all."

If you don't like the way women drive, get off the sidewalks.

I may not believe what you say but I'll defend to the death my right to criticize you for it.

Is your family happy? Or do you go home at night?

Be kind to your mother-in-law. Babysitters are expensive.

My mother-in-law is so nearsighted that she nagged a coat hanger for an hour.

When I first spotted you I thought my eyes were bad—I wish they were.

My mother-in-law is very neat. She puts paper under the cuckoo clock.

My wife is so neat. In the middle of the night I went to the kitchen for a drink. When I got back, the bed was made.

*Y*ours wasn't the first shotgun wedding—but I'll bet it was the first time the gun was held on the woman.

*M*adam, if a man loved you as much as you love you, it would be the greatest romance in history.

*W*hen my wife asked me to start a garden the first thing I dug up was an excuse.

I said to my wife, "Where do you want to go for your anniversary?"

She said, "I want to go somewhere I've never been before."

I said, "Try the kitchen."

I'll never forget the first time we met—but I'm trying.

His jokes are original, but the people who originated them died years ago.

My wife wanted her face lifted. They couldn't do that, but for $80 they lowered her body.

My wife went to the beauty parlor and got a mud pack. For two days she looked nice. Then the mud fell off.

*M*y wife was at the beauty parlor for two hours, and that was just for the estimate.

*N*ow my wife's on a diet of coconuts and bananas. She hasn't lost any weight, but can she climb a tree!

*M*y best friend ran away with my wife, and let me tell you, I miss him.

*G*od sneezed. What could I say to him?

A doctor told his patient to stop smoking. He added, "As long as you're quitting, I'll give you five bucks for your gold lighter."

I went to see a Beverly Hills analyst. He said, "Lie down and tell me everything." I did—and now he's doing my act.

This book has been bound
using handcraft methods, and
Smyth-sewn to ensure durability.

The dust jacket and interior were designed
by Christian Benton.
The text was edited by David Borgenicht.
The cover and interior were illustrated
by Wally Neibart.
The type was set in Gill Sans Medium
by Commcor Communications,
Philadelphia, Pennsylvania.